The Characters of Christmas
25 Family Devotionals for the Christmas Season

Steve Biddison

The Characters of Christmas

Published by Sword and Shield Publishing

Copyright © 2013 Steve Biddison

All Scripture quotations are taken from the Holy Bible, King James Version (KJV)

For more information, contact the author at
Stevebiddisonbooks@aol.com

ISBN-13: 978-1492909323

ISBN-10: 1492909327

DEDICATION

This book is dedicated first to my Father in Heaven and His Son Jesus Christ. Because of God's decision to send Jesus to earth, we now have the Christmas story.

Secondly, I want to dedicate this book to my family. It was during those early years of life, through my parents and grandparents, that the Christmas season became such a big part of my heritage. And to my wife and son, who continually help me carry out the spirit of Christmas. They were the original motivation behind writing this family devotional.

Christmas means age old beautiful music, family traditions and great memories...tears of joy and remembrance of those lost... and the promise because of His birth, the best gift ever, I will see them again in paradise.

Tracy Conchado Owens

The Christmas season initiates a moment for Believers to pause. We attempt to grasp the magnitude of God's love, the enormity of His power, and the depth of His humility. For some it is a time to cynically debate the virgin birth. For others it is a time to shop, spend, and go into debt. For others, like me, it is a time to be grateful for family and more than that, to bow on bended knee before the King.

Tina Webb, Author of *Before the Beginning*

Christmas means a time where the whole world looks to Christ, whether consciously or subconsciously, while experiencing a spirit of giving.

Corine Hyman, Author of *Why We Give Gifts at Christmas*

As people came from all around to see the Baby Jesus and to love Him, rejoice in Him, and follow Him, so do we as family and friends gather together to love, rejoice and celebrate, ultimately the very birth of Christ. It is such a special day. I know from experience that the love and passion for my family and friends just seems to be boundless during this time of the year. Of course, Jesus prefers us to celebrate Him every day and we should....by the way we live, love, talk & walk and rejoice. Christmas season is a time to partake in the very life of Jesus.

Beverly Noftsgar

Christmas is about the most amazing occurrence in history. Matthew wrote, "the virgin will be with child and will give birth to a son, and they will call him Immanuel, which means God is with us. (Matt. 1:23) What brought "Joy to the World" was Jesus coming to live with us AND to purchase our redemption so that we may have eternal life. No wonder we celebrate with family and gifts.

Ada Brownwell, Author of *Believing in Miracles Changes Your Future*

My grandmother made a nativity set in a ceramic class she took. It had all the people, sheep, camels, a wonderful earthtone patina. Some of the figures were almost a foot tall. My mother used to set it up every year and finally one year she gave it to me. Then we went through a series of financial disasters and geographic upheavals and the nativity set had to be left behind in a place we thought we could get back to, but never could recover it. I have learned through this and other experiences that Christ came into the world without a thing, had nowhere to lay His head during His life, and was laid in a borrowed tomb. All the physical things that people cherish during Christmas, none of those matter. Only Christ matters.

Mary Campagna Findley, Author of *Chasing the Texas Wind*

The joy of Christmas is the light in my children's eyes that no matter what we give them they are delighted and they can say "thank you Jesus" and find freedom in expressing their joy in the food, gifts, people playing with them, seeing family and having love showered on them... Christmas is being THE family and sharing with family

Danielle Ferrell

Christmas means family time at the Fury household for years. We gather Christmas Eve and day, enjoying good food and better company. These years there are a few empty seats at the family table. Faces and voices that are missing make the time we have together and even more precious.

I don't know how people that are not Christians make it through the holidays without the promise of a family homecoming – where there will be no faces missing and no sweet voices gone from the family circle.

Samantha Fury writes under the names, Samantha Fury and Samantha Lovern. She is the author of the fun, clean Christmas novel, *Maid For Martin.*

And she brought forth her firstborn son, and wrapped him in swaddling clothes, and laid him in a manger; because there was no room for them in the inn.

Luke 2:7

For God so loved the world, that he gave his only begotten Son, that whosoever believeth in him should not perish, but have everlasting life.

For God sent not his Son into the world to condemn the world; but that the world through him might be saved.

John 3:16-17

INTRODUCTION

Christmas has always been my favorite time of year. There is just something special about the house being decorated for the season, the lights glowing from buildings and houses around the city, the colder weather biting you each time you step outside, the Christmas carols sounding in every store you visit, and the excitement and anticipation that grows inside both children and adults alike as that special day approaches.

But Christmas brings more than just the glory we see and hear externally, it also changes the way we think and feel. Though it may not be a universal truth in everyone, most people are far more generous and giving during the Christmas season than at any other time of year. In addition, families usually spend more time together doing family things during the Christmas season than they do throughout the year. Christmas is special.

However, Christmas is special for a far deeper reason than the mass feelings of *peace on earth, good will towards men.* Christmas is special because it celebrates God's gift to humanity. Because of that gift, we can enjoy the decorations, lights, the carols, and our family. My desire in writing this devotional book is to not only bring the family together each day during this season, but give a way that we can keep the true meaning of Christmas at the forefront of our personal and family lives.

Each day, beginning with December 1st, each family unit can sit down together and not only look at each of the characters surrounding the story of Christmas, but discover what lessons or life applications we can learn from each one of them. This devotional also includes

discussion questions you can have with your family each day. It is your choice how deep you want to take it with your family.

Most of these devotionals are taken straight from the Biblical Christmas story. However, there are a few licenses I have taken in order to fit in with the traditional story of Christmas. For instance, we know historically that the wise men were not present at the actual birth of Jesus, but the traditional Christmas story always has them at the stable. So even though they are not literally a part of the actual historical Christmas, I am including them as one of the characters of Christmas. However, I am not including the secular renditions of Christmas like Santa, Rudolph, and Frosty. Those are tales for another time and cannot fit into these devotions.

Enjoy this Christmas season. And may you and your family be enriched by walking through this season with the characters of Christmas.

DECEMBER 1
GOD'S GIFT OF LOVE

Every Christmas, families all over the world give gifts to one another. In most all of these cases, they give these gifts because they love each other. I know when I was a child, I focused on those presents under the tree that had my name on it. Those were the ones that were most exciting to me. I would often pick up the presents when my parents weren't looking to feel the shape, estimate the weight, and in some unique situations hold it up in hopes of seeing through the paper. Why? I wasn't going to actually receive that gift until Christmas morning. But something inside the curiosity of a child compelled me to want to know what was inside that wrapping.

As I grew into my adult years, my focus changed from the gifts that I would receive to the gifts that I would be giving. Now my favorite part of Christmas morning is watching the anticipation and joy on my son's face as he receives his gifts. With each gift that he opens, my hope is that he can see how much his mother and I love him.

God is no different than we parents are. He wants nothing more than to prove to us how much He loves us by showering us with His blessings and His gift of love. He demonstrated that love to us a long time ago when He sent His Son to earth. He didn't have to send Jesus away from Heaven. But He chose to so that we could know His love. Think about how hard that would have been for Jesus. Before He came to earth, He was in Heaven and had everything. He was God. But then because He loved us, He did what God, the Father wanted and left that great place in Heaven and came down to earth to become a little baby and then grow up living as a boy and eventually a man. That is like one of us leaving our position on earth and choosing to become a bug to show the bugs how much we love them. Would any of us ever really choose to do that?

But God did. And by choosing to send Jesus to earth, God gave us the greatest example of how to give a gift because we love someone.

Family Discussion

What is your favorite part about the Christmas season? Why do you like that part so much?

In what ways can we show love to one another during this Christmas season?

In what ways can we show love to others outside of our family during this Christmas season?

December 2
Zechariah and Elisabeth: Keep on Praying

Not very long ago, we celebrated Thanksgiving. Thanksgiving was not just a day to gather around the table for a big turkey meal and watch some football. It was a day that we would focus on thanking God for all the blessings He has given to us and even thanking Him for answering those prayers and providing for us. God always wants to hear us thank Him for those things.

However, many times, we have not seen God's answer to those things we are praying for. It might be that someone in your family is sick and you have been praying for God to heal them. Or maybe someone is without a job and you are praying that God will give them a job. There is any number of things that you might have been praying for, but God has not answered.

As the New Testament begins its narrative leading up to the Christmas story, we see an old couple, Zechariah and Elisabeth who had been praying for decades that they would have a child. There was nothing wrong with that prayer. It's probably a better prayer than we pray sometimes about wanting God to give us certain toys, the latest electronics, or a new car. But for years their prayer went unanswered. It was not because God was punishing them or that they were not living right. The Bible explains that they were very godly people. In fact, their lives were so godly that they are an example to us on how to live our lives, even when we don't seem to get our prayers answered.

I am sure that this Christmas season there are things you have been praying for that God has not answered. Let me invite you during this time to learn three things that Zechariah and Elisabeth did during those many years of God not answering their prayers.

First, they **stayed faithful** to God. They did not give up on God because He was not answering their prayer. They continued serving God no matter what He had given or had not given them.

The second thing they did during their long wait to hear from God was **stay hopeful**. Despite years of unanswered prayer, they remained hopeful that one day God was going to answer their prayer. Their prayer probably went something like this, *God, You know the desires of our hearts and how we want You to answer our prayer for a child. But, Lord, I am willing to accept that You might not want to answer that prayer if it means You are going to get more glory out of us remaining childless. However, we will remain faithful and hopeful that You will grant it to us someday. If not, give us the grace to accept Your will. Amen.*

The third thing they did was **stay busy**. Zechariah and Elisabeth did not sit around moping and pouting during all those years they were not getting the answer to their prayers. They may not have gotten everything they wanted in life, but they were still doing what they could, where they could, for God.

Family Discussion

Can you think of anything we are or should be praying for right now?

We talked a little bit about staying faithful to God even when our prayers are not being answered. What does it mean to stay faithful?

Zechariah and Elisabeth stayed hopeful for many years that God would still answer their prayer. Are you staying hopeful that God will still answer your prayers or have you given up?

Zechariah and Elisabeth stayed busy doing work for God while they kept praying. How can we during this Christmas season do work for God? What can we do for God during the rest of the year?

December 3
Mary: The Lord's Servant
Luke 1:26-38

One of the greatest Christmas carols of all time is *Joy to the World.* We love to celebrate how great it was that "the Lord has come" and let "heaven and nature sing" all about the joys and happiness that the Christmas season brings to us. We see images scattered around the stores and in people's yards of that great Nativity scene with the baby Jesus in a manger with Joseph standing tall and Mary reclining with a look of perfect peace on her face.

But in that frozen image, how often do we take a step back and realize what both Mary and Joseph had to go through to get to that famous Nativity scene? Mary was most likely a young teenager when the Christmas story takes place. She probably had her whole life planned out in front of her. We know she was already engaged to Joseph, so she was most likely looking forward to her wedding and how she was going to decorate the house they would one day live in.

But then one day, all her plans came to a crashing halt when the angel Gabriel paid her a very important visit. He broke the news to her that she would soon become pregnant. Being that she was not yet married, she would certainly face a great deal of humiliation and disgrace. No girl at that time in history would ever dare get pregnant before she was married. However, Gabriel told her that she was a very special woman and that her pregnancy was a super-natural one. She would not be carrying just a normal baby. She would be carrying the Son of God whom God would send to earth for a very special reason.

Mary could have completely freaked out over this news. Not

only was it going to ruin her dream wedding, but she probably thought she would go down in history as the girl who cheated on her fiancé. But even in her young age, Mary responded in the most mature of ways, proving exactly why God had chosen her to be the mother of His Son. "I am the Lord's servant," she told the angel. "I am willing for this to come true."

Because of that wonderful example she set in her willingness to fully do what God wanted her to do, Mary has gone down in history as perhaps the most revered woman of all time.

Family Discussion

Have there been times in your life where you were asked to do something you really didn't want to do?

How did you respond?

Is that different than how God would have wanted you to respond?

December 4
Joseph: A Man of Integrity
Matthew 1:18-25

Around Christmas time, many parents tell their kids that they had better behave or Santa isn't going to bring them anything this year. We even sing a Christmas song that tells us that Santa is "making a list and checking it twice, gonna find out who's naughty or nice." Yet, somehow, every Christmas, those children receive gifts no matter if they had been naughty or nice. But what would happen one year if getting gifts really did depend on whether or not we had been naughty or nice? How many of us would know if we would receive gifts or go without that year? We might think we have been doing good, but were the bad things we did or the bad attitudes we had enough to keep us down? How would we know? How would God see us?

We know from the Bible that God thought Joseph was a really good guy. He was an honest, hard-working man who always tried to do the right thing. In addition, Joseph was engaged to be married to the woman he loved. God saw Joseph as the perfect person to be the earthly father for God's Son, Jesus. It was God's perfect plan to bring Mary, the woman He wanted to be the mother of the Christ child, and Joseph, the hard working, honest man that God wanted to be the earthly father for His Son, together.

I want you to think just for a minute about how much of a miracle it was not necessarily that God brought them together, but that He kept them together. When Joseph found out that Mary was pregnant without being married to him, it was within his right in that culture to have her killed or at least publically humiliated. Most men back then would have done that. And believe me, Joseph thought about it. But he also loved Mary and didn't want to ruin the rest of her life so instead of publically embarrassing her to the point that she would never be able to live a normal life, he decided he would just send her away so no one would know that she was pregnant. That single act alone, speaks volumes of what kind of man Joseph was. He knew that, even though it was his right to do, he was not going to embarrass Mary.

However, God still had the plans to keep those two together and so He sent an Angel to come to the rescue once again. The Angel filled Joseph in on God's plan and told him that God had caused Mary to get pregnant and He still wanted Joseph to marry her. Even though Joseph still probably felt a little strange marrying a woman who was already pregnant, he once again did the right thing, obeyed God, and took Mary to be his wife.

Family Discussion

How do we know Joseph was a man of integrity (how do we know he was nice, not naughty)?

Have you seen times when people were making fun of or putting down someone else? How would you feel if that was happening to you?

Because he was such a good man, God chose Joseph for a very special job, being the earthly father for Jesus. How can you show God that you are ready for any job He might have for you?

December 5
Gabriel: God's Messenger

Even in our very secular, non-Christian society we live in, one of the wonderful things about the Christmas season is that the name of Jesus is heard more often than any other time of year. You cannot go into too many places of business where you don't hear Christmas songs being played over their speaker system. Nativity scenes are in both yards and in many places of business. Yes, quite often we hear songs about Santa Claus and Rudolph, but mixed into all those songs, we will also hear *Silent Night* and *Hark, The Herald Angels Sing.*

I know many people argue that Christmas seems more about presents and Santa Claus than it does about Jesus. In many ways, they are right. However, I challenge you to look on the positive side of things. The name and story of Jesus is proclaimed throughout the world during the Christmas season. And God promises that His Word does not go out into the world without accomplishing a purpose. So instead of being upset about how much Christmas has moved away from the story of Jesus, let's celebrate that His name is being talked about. In fact, let's do more than just celebrate it. Let's be a part of it by making sure we proclaim God's message to our world.

The angel, Gabriel, gave the first message concerning Christmas when he spoke to Mary telling her that she was going to have a child. Although, we do not know for sure that it was Gabriel that told Joseph not to be afraid to take Mary as his wife, we do know that it was an angel of the Lord. Even if it wasn't Gabriel, he was doing the same thing that Gabriel did. He gave a message from God to the human race.

As we examine the idea of Gabriel being a messenger, there are many things that we as humans can learn. First, Gabriel was obedient to God. It's not always easy doing what God tells us to do. I'm sure at first Gabriel did not particularly look forward to breaking the news to Mary that she was going to be pregnant, knowing that it might scare her to death. Nor was it easy telling Joseph that the woman he loved was pregnant and that he should not be upset about it. But Gabriel was a great example of being obedient to God by telling them anyway.

Second, we see Gabriel specifically trying to calm their fears. He tells them not to be afraid. Those of us who have read the Bible, or even heard the Christmas story told over and over again, might have a tendency to just pass over this part as if Gabriel was just saying hello. But think about it for a minute. If an angel suddenly appeared in front of you, wouldn't you be afraid? And how would you feel if he told you something pretty scary like he told Mary and Joseph? I bet we would all admit that we would probably be afraid. I am sure Gabriel didn't just tell them to not be afraid. He most likely spoke in a very reassuring voice that helped calm their fears down and allowed them to trust and believe that the news he was giving them was good. Wouldn't it be great if we could all learn to speak to each other, and the people we encounter each day, that same way. How much more peace in our families and in our world would we see if everyone learned to speak like Gabriel with a tone that causes all doubts and fears to subside?

Family Discussion

What kind of message does God want you to give to the other members of your family?

What kind of message does God want you to give to the people you see
regularly?

How can we as a family speak to one another that does not cause fear,
doubt, or anxiety?

December 6
John: Excitement for Jesus
Luke 1:39-45

As a child, Christmas morning was my favorite day of year. I was so excited for Christmas morning to come that I quite often had trouble sleeping Christmas Eve. I would lay in bed anticipating the joys of opening my presents the next morning. In my family, we were never allowed to just get up and open our gifts whenever we wanted to. We had a set a routine and a preset time when the family would gather together in the living room to open the presents. However, that did not stop me from getting up long before that hour so I could just sit in the living room and anticipate the coming morning. I remember early one Christmas around 4:00 in the morning; I had awakened with that same excitement I had every Christmas morning before that. Quietly, I made my way down the hall where I took out a book that I had received as a gift the night before at a larger family Christmas Eve gathering and began to read it, hoping to get lost in the book so the remaining four hours would pass quickly. I had only been reading for about half of an hour when I heard my father's footsteps coming down the hall. I tried to explain to him that I was too excited to sleep, but I was sent back to my bed anyway. But even in bed, my excitement for the next morning never subsided.

As I was once again reading the Christmas story, I was struck with the realization that even in the time leading up to the very first Christmas; children were excited about what was going to happen on Christmas morning. While Mary was pregnant with Jesus, she went to visit her relative, Elisabeth. Remember, Elisabeth was the one who for decades could not have any children, but God had promised her and her husband, Zechariah, that even in their old age, they would finally have a child. And now at the time Mary was visiting, Elisabeth was about six months pregnant.

When Mary entered Elisabeth's house, John, the baby inside Elisabeth, somehow recognized that the baby inside Mary was God's Son. We are told that John started jumping up and down in excitement. That simple verse in the Christmas story speaks volumes to how we should all be living our lives. Even as an unborn baby, John recognized when God was at work. How often do we recognize when God is at work in our lives and in the world around us? God has not changed. He still works. We just often don't recognize His work because we are tuned into other things.

In the unborn baby, John, we also see a rush of excitement simply because He saw God's plan unveiling. I know that many of us want to feel that excitement at seeing God in action, but for some reason we seldom, if ever, get that feeling. Is it possible that we have grown stale in our view of God and we no longer view it as an exciting thing when someone comes to know Him in a personal way? Is it possible that we do not feel that excitement when God provides for us because we are used to it happening. Have we grown so used to God working everything out that we no longer feel the excitement of those every day miracles?

I challenge you this Christmas season to purposefully open your eyes and hearts to see all the things that God is doing around you. I guarantee you that God has not stopped working. We are just too busy in our own world to recognize God's work. And secondly, I challenge you to get excited about even the little things that God does. I believe if we get excited about those things and thank Him for what He does, He will open our eyes to see even bigger things that He is doing. Give it a try. See what happens.

Family Discussion

What do you get excited about?

What are some of the areas around you that you see that God has done or is doing something?

What does God have to do to get your excited about seeing His work?

December 7
Elisabeth – Not Deserving, But Grateful
Luke 1:39-45

Every so often, you open a Christmas present that is a total surprise and might even make you wonder whether or not you even deserve that gift. It was so much more than you had imagined you would get. But hopefully you have had that experience at once in your life. I remember when I was about 8 or 9 years old opening what was for me at the time, my favorite present I had ever received. I could not believe that I actually had one. I am purposefully not telling you what it was because you knowing it now would lose the impact of the story. Let's just say that though it was rare at that time for a kid my age to own one, in the next decade it became so common that everyone had one and now it has come full circle where almost no one has one anymore because better things have come out. But for me then, it was the best gift imaginable and I knew I did not deserve it. But my parents knew how much I would love it.

It would be wonderful if we all felt that way every Christmas morning. Just think how grateful we would be if we viewed all of God's blessings as something we don't deserve, but He gives it to us anyway. Elisabeth, the same woman we have read about before, demonstrated this kind of attitude when Mary came to visit her. Here she was the talk of the town. The walking miracle. The woman who was six months pregnant after many decades of never having a child. It would have been so easy for her to think that she deserved to have a child. After all, she had served the Lord faithfully for a very long time. She could have thought that this was God's reward for her faithful living.

But she never felt that way. In fact, when Mary came to visit her, her very words shows that she knew she did not deserve the many blessings she was seeing. "What have I done to deserve to have the mother of my Lord come for a visit?"

Wouldn't it be great if more people had the same attitude? If more people felt like they did not deserve the blessings they were given? Do you think they would be more grateful for the things they do have if they didn't feel like they deserved them?

Family Discussion

Is there any great thing you have that you do not feel like you deserve?

Let's take a few minutes and go around the room, giving once sentence prayers thanking God for the things He has done that go beyond what we really deserve?

December 8
Mary: The Girl Who Knew God's Word
Luke 1:46-53

For me, the Christmas season does not start with the decorating of the Christmas tree, hanging the lights on the house, or even buying Christmas presents. Even as a child, I did not feel that proverbial Christmas spirit just because the stores doubled the number of aisles they had dedicated to toys. In my mind, there was only one thing that ushered in the Christmas season – the music. Maybe that was because in my family, we made a big deal about pulling down the Christmas albums from the top shelf and putting the music on as we readied ourselves to decorate the tree. My mom and dad chose the Christmas albums we listened to and their favorite was one by Bing Crosby. I don't think we could even decorate the Christmas tree without the baritone crooning of Bing Crosby's voice echoing through our living room. And even though living in central Texas, we never had a chance of snow coming in December, we could always sing, "I'm Dreaming of a White Christmas." And that was one of those magical things about Christmas. We could always dream that what we were singing could really come true.

I do have to admit that as a child, I preferred the non-religious Christmas songs over the religious ones. I'm sure most kids are the same. It was much more fun to sing *Jingle Bells* or *Santa Claus is Coming to Town* than it was *O Holy Night*. But sometime in the midst of those years crossing from childhood to adulthood, my preference for Christmas music completely changed. Now for me, no Christmas playlist is complete without *Silent Night, O Holy Night,* and *Joy to the*

World.   However, as much as I now love those classic religious Christmas carols, I have found that so many of them are not completely based on the Bible.   And even though I will use some of those traditional stories, though not biblical ones, in this Christmas devotional; I will point out that there was no such character in the Bible as the innkeeper or the little drummer boy.   But even more surprising than those two examples, not only did the wise men never show up at the manger scene, but contrary to what tradition tells us, we have no idea if there were three of them.   I am not sure why these stories have been included into the traditional story of Christmas, but I am kind of okay with it.   I assume that perhaps those writing the songs did not really know their Bible that well.   But I have to give them credit for trying.   They could have written another song about a reindeer with a glowing nose.

However, the very first ever Christmas song did not stray from the Bible.   It was sung by the very mother-to-be of Jesus when she visited Elisabeth.   Elisabeth had just greeted her and Mary suddenly broke out in song, praising God for not just the mighty work He had done in her and was going to do for the world, but her song also conjured up images from the Old Testament from such places as Genesis, Job, Psalms, and Isaiah.   It showed how that even as very young teenage girl, she knew and understood the Scriptures.

In order to fully appreciate her understanding of the Old Testament, we need to remember that during those days where the role of women was considerably different than it is today, Mary probably did not even know how to read.   Therefore, she could not study the Bible on her own.   She had probably learned and memorized it by listening to the teachings of her father.   But it had to have gone much deeper than that. She treasured the Word of God as the most important thing to her and then lived it out in front of everyone. As a result of her love, faith, and devotion to Him, God chose her to be the mother of His Son.

We have it so much easier in today's world to learn and understand the Bible. Whereas Mary couldn't even read it and a few generations ago, there might have only been one Bible per family, now days we don't even have to carry a Bible with us in order to read it. Many of us already have it downloaded on our phones or tablets. And if we don't have it, all you have to do is find internet access and you can read it from one of many different translations. We are without excuse when it comes to knowing what God says. But for many of us, we never take that deeper step. We never let the Word of God transport from our minds to our hearts to our lives. Maybe this Christmas season would be a good time to start letting the Bible change your life.

Family Discussion

What is your favorite religious Christmas song? Why?

Tell us one story from the Bible that you like. Why do you like it?

What can we learn from that story?

What can we as a family do this Christmas season to show our love, faith, and devotion to God?

December 9
Caesar: God Even Uses Bad to Accomplish Good.
Luke 2:1-2

There are many people who think it is their job to point out to everyone everything that is wrong with Christmas. They will point out how commercialized and materialistic Christmas has become in our society as well as reminding us how much the concept of Santa has at times stolen the true meaning of Christmas away from the season. And then there are those who do not like many of the traditions of Christmas, even the season itself, because so many of those traditions have their roots in paganism.

Although in most all of those cases they are right, I find it sad that those who stand so strong against Christmas rob themselves of so many of the joys that God intends us to experience each Christmas season. Yes, it is true that so many of the Christmas traditions may have had non-Christian origins, but that does not mean we have to ignore them. God can use such things as the Christmas tree, exchanging of gifts, putting lights on the house, etc. to teach us how to live His way. I bet God can even use the legends of Santa, Rudolph, and Frosty to teach us valuable life lessons. That is the way God is. He can turn what is often meant for evil into something that works for His good.

At the time in history when Jesus was born, the Jews were ruled by the Roman Empire and were not always treated fairly. In fact, they had been waiting for God to send them the Messiah to deliver them from the Romans who were ruled by a man named Caesar Augustus. In the Jews eyes, the rule of Caesar was one of the dark times for their people.

At the time of the Christmas story, Caesar had summoned everyone back to their home town so they could be counted and taxed. No one really wanted to make that journey just so they could pay more money to the government. But that was Caesar's order. However, what we sometimes fail to realize is that God often brings evil people into a place of power so that He can accomplish His goals. Hundreds of years before, God had said that the Messiah would be born in Bethlehem. However, Mary and Joseph did not live in Bethlehem. But since God already knew that, He made it so that Caesar would come into power and require them to go to Bethlehem just at the very moment that Mary was to give birth to Jesus. If God used the evil Caesar to bring about God's good, then don't you think He can still use that which is not good in our world and make it used for good?

Family Discussion

Let's look at some of the traditions of Christmas that did not come from the Bible and see if there is a way God wants us to use it for good or teach us valuable life lessons

Examples: The Christmas tree, Christmas lights, exchanging gifts, Santa Claus, Rudolph, etc.

December 10
The Donkey: Helping Others in Need

The holiday cheer that spreads through the Christmas season often brings out the best in some people. You hear stories of people in line at the grocery store paying for other people's groceries when they saw that they could not afford it. At nearly every Walmart entrance you see people giving to help the poor and needy. Others fill up shoeboxes to send to kids in third world countries and some give to children whose parents are in prison. With all the greed and materialism that surrounds Christmas, there is the other side that demonstrates that there are still good people in this world who truly want to help others.

We see this great trait of helping others in the traditional story of Mary riding on the back of a donkey for up to four days from Nazareth to Bethlehem. In reality, the Bible does not tell us she rode a donkey nor do we know how long they were in Bethlehem before she gave birth. But since we are looking at the traditional stories and characters of the Christmas story, the donkey gives us a great example of letting go of our own comfort to help others who are in greater need. Let's face it, even for a donkey, carrying a woman nine months pregnant for four days has got to be a little uncomfortable. But let's pretend like he knew that for the betterment of the world, he would have to sacrifice his own comfort. What an example that is to us today! Are we at least as good as that donkey was? Don't let a donkey's self-sacrifice beat us out in the area of helping others. Christmas is a great time of year to begin making a real effort to help others out.

Family Discussion

What are some of the ways you can help someone during this Christmas season?

What can our family do to help others?

Who are some people we can help and how can we help them?

December 11
The Innkeepers Who Said No:
Turning Away Christ

Although we do not really know from the Bible anything about the innkeepers who turned Mary and Joseph away, or if there really were any of those innkeepers, but the traditional story of Christmas would not be complete without the telling of Joseph going from inn to inn, from hotel to hotel, trying to find a room for the very pregnant Mary. And one by one, each of the innkeepers regrettably shook their head and told them that he had no room for them.

I'm sure that had they known the baby Mary was carrying was the Son of God and that He would be born that night, they would have found some way to make room for them. Maybe the innkeeper would have given up his bed or one of his children's rooms for the night. After all, that family would go down in history as owning the place that Jesus was born in. But no one, other than Mary and Joseph, knew that the Son of God would be born that night. So one by one, all the innkeepers turned them away because they had no room at the inn.

People today are not all that different. God continually knocks on the doors of people's hearts and He keeps getting the same answer that Joseph received a few thousand years ago. They have no room for Him. Just as I am sure that had the innkeeper truly understood that God's Son was to be born that night, he would have made room for them, I am just as sure that most people, if they truly understood who God was and what the future without Him would look like, they would let Him into their heart and lives. But they don't.

Most the people we will come in contact with during our lifetime will not have let God in. They may not be bad people. The innkeepers who turned away Mary and Joseph were not bad people. They just did not know the whole truth of what was happening.

It is our job to tell the people we know the truth about who Jesus really is. This Christmas season is a great time to do that because most the people we know are celebrating the baby Jesus. But the baby Jesus is not the whole story. Jesus was sent to earth as a baby to grow up, live a perfect life, and one day die for our sins. That is the truth behind the Christmas story.

So while we run about our daily lives in this busiest time of year, slow down just enough to think about all the people who are out shopping for Christmas presents who probably don't fully understand why Jesus really came to earth. And even though God has probably knocked on their heart's door many times, they have continued to turn him away because they had no room for Him in the inn of their heart.

Family Discussion

Who are some of the people you know who have not yet let Christ into their lives?

What do you think we can do to help them see the truth about God?

Why do you think people don't let Christ into their lives?

December 12
The Stable:
Making The Best Out of Life

Have you ever wanted something and couldn't find it anywhere? For you parents, it might have been a Christmas gift you wanted to get one of your children and yet it was sold out in every store you went to. For some of you it might have been the newest video game or even phone. It was such a hot item that every place was sold out. And then maybe through the frantic disappointment, you finally found one place that had the item still available. Do you remember the relief and excitement you felt when you finally got it?

That was the kind of feeling that Mary and Joseph must have felt in the traditional telling of the Christmas story. After searching long and hard for a place to stay, and being turned down by every innkeeper in Bethlehem, they finally found an innkeeper who volunteered to give them the stable out back.

Most of us today would have complained bitterly with such bad accommodations. It was not ideal and probably smelled like hay and animals. Mary and Joseph could have complained about it. But they didn't. Instead, they made the best out of their situation. They probably moved all the loose hay together in one area and made a decently comfortable mattress. It may not have been the Hilton Hotel, but it was a roof over their head. They knew the alternative was sleeping out in the streets with all the other people who didn't have a place to stay. At least this way, they had a little privacy while Jesus was born.

Unfortunately today, many people don't know how to make the best of their situations. They want the newest and the best of everything and complain if they don't have it. But God wants us to learn to make the best in whatever situation He has us in. It may not always be the greatest and the best, but God looks out more for our future than our present. Think what the story of Christmas would have been like had the innkeeper at the first Holiday Inn they went to had given them a room. It would make for a rather uninteresting Christmas story. But since Jesus was born in a backyard stable amongst all the animals, we now have a great Christmas story that is told over and over.

Family Discussion

Why do you think God wants us to make the best out of whatever circumstances we are in?

As you think about circumstances you and your family are in right now, what can you do to make sure that you are making the best out of your life situations?

During this Christmas season, how can you as a family show that you are grateful to God for the things He has given you?

December 13
The Animals in the Stable:
Witnesses to a Miracle

Virtually every Nativity scene we see in stores, in people's yards, or in pictures, we see animals surrounding Mary, Joseph, and Jesus. Combining those images with the traditional stories of that famous night, we almost get the impression that the animals were willingly moved out of their normal sleeping place so that Jesus could be born. Although the Bible never mentions the animals or a stable, only a manger or feeding trough, we are going to assume for the sake of the story that the animals were indeed present.

Think about what they must have thought that night. They were settling in for what they thought would be just a normal night. But then their owner brought two people to their stable. They must have recognized right away that the woman was pregnant and probably heard her tell her husband that she would probably deliver that night. So they graciously moved aside and that night witnessed the most amazing event in earth's history. Of course, I put words and thoughts into the animals during this description, but I wonder how many of us step aside from our own hectic life to watch God work in miraculous ways. Think about it. Has God stopped doing wonderful and even miraculous things? Or are we too busy doing life that we don't slow down enough to observe the work that God is doing all around us.

In this part of the traditional Christmas story, we can learn from those cows, sheep, donkeys, and whatever other animal might have been around. When they were forced out of their normal routine of life, they could have chosen to be upset, perhaps even walked away to go pout under a tree somewhere. But they recognized that God was about to do something very special and they wanted to witness this great event. Would you make that same choice if you were forced out of your comfort and routine? Instead of recognizing that God was at work, too many of us would walk away upset and therefore miss witnessing the move of God.

Family Discussion

Has there been a time that you were forced to leave something you were used to doing? How did it make you feel?

Has there been a time that you have witnessed a true miracle and move of God? Tell about it.

What can you do to make yourself more attentive to seeing God's work around you?

This Christmas season, what can we do as a family that will help us see God's work?

December 14
The Heavenly Hosts: Declaring Christ
Luke 2:8-14

For me, the Christmas season would not be complete without hearing Manheim Steamroller's Christmas collection. I love the arrangements of so many of the popular Christmas carols. There are a few that have always stood out as some of my favorites. One of them is *Hark, The Herald Angels Sing.* I could listen to that song a couple of hundred times each Christmas season as in my heart I sing in worship, "Glory to the newborn King."

It must have been an incredible sight when scores of Angels appeared in the night sky outside Bethlehem declaring "peace on earth and mercy mild, God and sinners reconciled." Can you imagine what it would have been like to be there to hear the choir of angels singing, "Hail the Heaven born prince of peace. Hail the Son of Righteousness?"

I know the angels had a job to do. They were sent to tell the shepherds to go find the new born baby Jesus. But I do not think they looked at it as just a job. They saw it as an incredible privilege that they were chosen to be the first to announce to the world that God's Son had been born. For those angels in the sky that night, it must have been the happiest day of their lives and there is no doubt that when they sang that night, their joy and excitement was evident and at an all-time high.

Down through the ages, we still get a small glimpse of that excitement each Christmas season. Yes, there is still the hustle and bustle of Christmas decorating, shopping, and parties. There is still the draw so many children have to Santa and the excitement of hoping to catch a glimpse of Rudolph's nose glowing in the night sky on Christmas Eve. For some, there is still the worry about how they will pay for everything they bought during the Christmas season. But in the midst of all the commotion, the joy of Christmas still rings out as more than any other time of year, the name of Jesus is spoken. And I know that brings a smile to God's heart. For His desire today is the same as it was that night so long ago when the angels appeared in the night sky saying they brought good news that will bring joy to the earth. He still desires there to be peace to those who find God's favor.

Family Discussion

Why was Christ's birth such big news that a squad of angels had to sing about it (feel free to dig deeper into this question with older children – beyond the Christmas story).

How can we experience peace in our lives?

The angels were very excited about announcing the birth of Jesus. In what ways can we show that kind of excitement for God?

December 15
God: Meeting People Where They Are
Luke 2:1-20

Every community and every school has those people that are undesirable. Not too many people want to hang around them. Maybe we feel they are way beneath us or maybe there are legitimate reasons to stay away from them (like maybe they just plain smell bad). Sometimes we feel sorry for those people and other times we feel disgust. Sometimes they can't help the way they are and other times it seems like they go out of their way to rub people the wrong way. Do you know those kinds of people? It is natural to want to stay away from them. But what would have happened if God had viewed us like that? Face it, compared to a perfect God, we are those undesirable people.

In this very familiar section of the Bible read every Christmas season, we see how God brought Joseph and Mary to the town of Bethlehem, where it was prophesied the Messiah would be born. Since Joseph's family had been from Bethlehem, he had to return there for the census ordered by Caesar Augustus.

While they were there, Mary went into labor. There were no hospitals then and since this was census time, there were no empty rooms in any of the motels. The best place Mary and Joseph could find was an old barn. It was there, that she gave birth to the King of kings.

Meanwhile, in a nearby field, there were shepherds watching their flock of sheep. They were minding their own business and probably passing the time telling stories. Then an angel appeared to them and told them that the Savior had just been born and they would find Him in a stable in Bethlehem. After making that proclamation, the angel was joined by a multitude of other angels who were singing and praising God for showing His love to the world.

As much as we think we know how much God loves our world, we cannot come even close to understanding, much less imitating the love that God has for His world. If only we could love like God loves! But the best we can do is hope to give just a reflection of His love. It's a good thing God gave us an example of His love so that we might learn to reflect that love to our world.

The first thing God did to show His love to us is **to meet us where we were**. He did not wait for the world to come to Him. He came to the world as a human. He did not demand that we reach to His level to find that love. He came to our level. He wants the same thing from us in our home, our work, our school, and in our world. If we want to show love to our world, then we must go where they are and spend time with them. Jesus did that for us. We should follow His example and do it to others.

Family Discussion

Are there undesirable people around you?

How do you think God wants you to react to them?

What are some very specific things you can do to reach out and show God's love to the people who are not like you?

December 16
The Shepherds: Experiencing God

As we get older in life, many of us start making what is called our "bucket list." It's those things we want to do or see sometime before we "kick the bucket" or before we die. We may or may not actually make a physical list, but in our heads we have that list. I have several places I want to visit some time in my lifetime and probably will not ever get to cross them all of my list. However, recently I was able to see one of the places on my bucket list. For some reason, I had always wanted to walk through *The Garden of the Gods*. But I could never justify taking vacation days and vacation money to go to Colorado Springs just to spend a few hours walking among big rocks. However, by God's grace and provision, my job sent me to Denver for a few weeks and I was able to spend a day in Colorado Springs walking in *The Garden of the Gods*. What an amazing picture of God's creativity in His creation! Being so much in awe at the sights, I snapped hundreds of pictures and put together a video slide show of that park because I wanted to share my experience with the world.

My sense of amazement at seeing *The Garden of the Gods* pales in comparison to what the shepherds felt the night the angels appeared to them. They saw and heard the closest thing that a human can get to experiencing the glory of God. As a result of what they had witnessed, they immediately left their sheep, quite possibly losing their jobs afterwards, to run into Bethlehem to find the Christ child.

Other than Mary and Joseph, the shepherds were the first humans to see God's Son as a living human being. What an incredible experience. After that night, they had nothing left on their bucket list. They had seen the most glorious of glories and from there ran to tell everyone they came in contact with that the Christ had been born in a manger in Bethlehem.

Although we may not be able to have quite the same wonderful experience as the shepherds had that Christmas night, there are many ways we can experience God today. With the Holy Spirit now residing inside of us, we are just a connection with Him away from experiencing God inside our own hearts.

In the middle of all the busyness that engulfs the Christmas season, find some time to sit quietly and ask God to show Himself real and personal to you. Pray, worship, meditate, read the Bible. But perhaps most importantly, sit back and listen to God.

Family Discussion

What are some of the things you want to see or do sometime in your life?

How would you have felt if you were one of the shepherds that night when the angels appeared?

What does it mean to you to experience God?

December 17
The Little Drummer Boy:
Giving Your Best to God

One of my favorite Christmas stories (actually it is a song) is *The Little Drummer Boy.* Now I know that this story is not a story you will find in the Bible, but it does fit in with the Biblical story of Jesus. I don't really know why I like that song so much. Perhaps it is because it tells the tale of someone who didn't have anything to offer to a king, but a talent he had for playing the drum. But so often as I listen to different renditions of that song, my mind's eye sees so much more to the story than the song portrays. I see a poor boy who gives his talent to the Son of God and Jesus not only smiles at him, but from that day on begins to bless him. I picture this boy growing up through all the ages of human history, playing his drum. I see him in marching bands and I see him as a drummer on the battlefield. I see him playing his drum on the worship team at his church and I see him playing his drum during military salutes of fallen comrades. And each time he plays, he sees Jesus still smiling at him.

I feel that many of us can relate to that young shepherd boy. We really may not have anything magnificent to offer to God, but if we give to Him the little bit that we have, He will smile at us. If we use our talent to honor Him, He will bless us. And just like in my vision of what the little drummer boy became in his life, God will continue to smile on us as we use what He has given us to honor Him.

Family Discussion

In the story of the little drummer boy, why do you think we are told Jesus smiled at him?

What talent can you give to Jesus?

What other ways do you feel like you can serve God?

December 18
The Star: The Guide Through Life
Matthew 2:1-2

While I was in elementary school, every year my school would put on a Christmas program. There would be a choir that sang Christmas songs to go along with skits that celebrated Christmas. Those programs are still very special memories to me as I usually auditioned for some part in the skit. Even in my young years, I felt like I wanted to be a star in the program. Some people were very happy to stand on the risers and get lost in the numbers that was the choir. Not me. I wanted people to see me. I wanted to be the star. The funny thing is, I didn't really want those parts so that I could be popular or that others would say great things about me. It's a good thing too that those weren't my motivations, because I never achieved that. But I wanted those speaking lines because I wanted my family to see me. I wanted them to feel it was worth their while to come to a school Christmas program for more than just getting to see my standing on risers surrounded by dozens of other kids. And the only way I knew they could see me was if I had one of those "starring" parts.

As egotistical as it might sound, those desires of being the star of my elementary school Christmas program make me think a little bit about the Star of Bethlehem. Stepping out of the Biblical timeline to accommodate the traditional story of Christmas, we see three very wise philosophers, from a land very far away from Bethlehem, notice an unusual star in the sky. Seeing it come up night after night, they began to do research into what that star might mean. They soon determined that the star was a sign that a king had been born. But not just any king got a star. This must have been a very special king. So off they went to follow the star to find that king that was so special.

We all know what was so special about that king. He was the Son of God. But what about the star? What made it so special?

1. The star pointed the way to Jesus. The wise men could never have found Jesus had it not been for this very special star leading the way.

2. The star was seen at just the right time in history. God knew when to send the star so that the wise men would see it and follow it.

3. The star's story has been told for centuries. And every time it is told, we think about Jesus coming to earth.

Family Discussion

In what ways can you be like the star and help point others to find Jesus?

Can you think of how things you do right now to be God's star can make a difference all through your life?

December 19
The Wise Men: What Made Them Wise?

Nearly every Christmas nativity scene we see set up during the Christmas season has Mary and Joseph surrounded not only by the animals and the shepherds, but by three wise men bearing gifts to the newborn King. Where that might make for a great scene with the poor and lowly shepherds and the rich and powerful magi bowing together before the Christ child, that is not the way it really played out. Most scholars believe that those wise men, however many there really were, probably arrived two years after that first Christmas night.

However, despite the historic inaccuracy of the traditional Christmas story, we still associate the visit by the wise men with Christmas morning. And though we do not really know much about them, we do know that they were wise. The traditional and famous Christmas carol, *We Three Kings,* refers to them in some kind of royal capacity. Others call them Magi. All we really know is that they came from the east (possibly as far away as China) following a star until they came to the house where Mary, Joseph, and Jesus were living. But despite the fact that we have very limited knowledge of them, we can deduce that they were indeed wise.

First, they were wise because they followed God's leading. They knew enough about God and prophecies that when this glorious star appeared to them, they knew it was a sign of God that the true King has been born.

Later when appearing before Herod, they were wise enough to realize that despite what Herod said, his only goal was to kill Jesus.

Secondly, we see that they were wise because they looked for

Jesus for the right reasons. Whereas Herod wanted to find Jesus in order to kill him, the wise men wanted to find Jesus so they could worship Him. They were wise enough to know that Jesus was a special gift from God and deserved the worship that they would give Him.

Much of the world pretends to seek Jesus during the Christmas season. But unfortunately, they are seeking the story of the baby in the manger and not the King of kings who died to save us.

Finally, we see them being wise in the fact that they left the comforts and riches of their home, giving up everything, in order to find Jesus. It was most likely a two year journey that they went on just to find Jesus. That in itself tells us all we need to know about who these men were.

Family Discussion

This Christmas season, how can we be wise like the wise men and follow God?

What reasons do you follow Jesus? What reasons should we follow Jesus?

What is it that God wants you to give to Him this Christmas season?

December 20
Herod: The Grinch Who Tried To Steal Christmas

Every Christmas, the deep baritone voice of Thurl Ravenscroft echoes from television sets across the country singing, "You're a mean one, Mr. Grinch." The song immediately reminds us of the green oddly shaped creature who hated Christmas so much that he tried to sneak down to Whoville and kill Christmas for all the little Whos who lived in Whoville.

Of course the green, cat-like figure of Mr. Grinch is a fictional character Dr. Seuss invented to show that the true spirit of Christmas can melt even the hardest and coldest heart. But a few thousand years ago, there really was a Grinch that tried to steal Christmas. He wasn't green with skin color, but he was green with envy when the wise men told them that a new king had been born. This Grinch's name was Herod and he was the ruler that now felt threatened that a new king had been born.

Most of us know the story of how he asked the wise men to tell him where the new king was so that he could go worship him too. But they were wise enough to understand that Herod really wanted to kill Jesus so they never went back and told him where Jesus was.

Herod hated the idea of a new king being born that he made it a law that every boy who was two years old or younger had to be put to death. Thankfully, Mary and Joseph listened to God and left the area before Herod's men could kill Jesus. Of course, God would not have allowed that to happen, but had Herod been successful in his attempts to kill the new king, then the story of Christmas would have been killed and just like the Grinch had tried to do with the Whos, Christmas would have been ruined and we would not be celebrating it still today.

But of course, God would not allow that to happen because the story of Christmas is more than just a story about a baby being born. It is the beginning of the greatest story ever told – a story of how God became man and sacrificed Himself so that people even thousands of years later might live.

And even though the true message of Christmas is often times hidden behind the mask of Frosty, Santa, and Rudolph, God will not allow the story and message of Christmas to be killed. Because in that story, we have hope and we have life. Because of Christmas, Christ came into the world to live the perfect life and die in payment for our sins. And no Grinch can ever stop that story.

Family Discussion

What ways do we see today that some people might still be trying to kill Christmas?

Think back through this Christmas season. What are some of the symbols that are visible in stores, in people's houses, and around town that still portray the true meaning of Christmas?

What are some of the things we can do as a family to make sure that the truth of Christmas stays alive?

December 21
Gaspar and the Gift of Gold

The Bible doesn't give us a lot of information about the wise men. We don't even know that there were only three of them. There may have been more. But tradition tells us that there were three and in some stories passed down through the ages, the wise men are even given names. Although there is no reason to truly believe that these names are true, for the sake of our story, we are going to pretend that they are.

Gaspar was the name of one of the wise men. According to tradition, he came from India to seek the newborn king who had been promised by God in the stars. He brought a gift of gold to give to Jesus. At that time gold was something you offered to a king. Gaspar and his friends knew that this was no ordinary baby. He was the King of Kings and they needed to show him that kind of respect.

Gaspar and his friends are sometimes referred to as the three kings who came to worship Jesus. Even though they were rich, powerful, and famous in their own world, they volunteered to leave that luxury to go see a new king that they knew was superior to them. They were willing to give up their power, riches, and everything they held dear in order to submit themselves to Jesus.

Today Christmas is a great season because so many do acknowledge Jesus. They talk about Him, they speak or sing His name, and many go to church for the first time since Easter. But sadly, so many stop right there. They see Him mainly as a baby in the manger with a passing thought that this is God's Son that we are celebrating. Unlike, Gaspar, the wise man, many people never fully realize that Jesus is not just a cute baby that we celebrate every December. The Christmas story is not just a fun story to tell our children while we talk about peace on earth and good will towards man. They do not honor Him is the royal King of universe that He is.

So what will you bring to Jesus this Christmas season? Gaspar brought a gift of gold to show Jesus that he knew that Jesus was the King.

Family Discussion

We may not have a gift of gold we can give, but how can we show Jesus as well as show the world that we know that He is the King?

Gaspar gave up is fame, power, and riches to find Jesus. Is God asking you to give up anything so that Jesus can reign as King in your life?

Christmas morning is just a few days away. What do you think we as a family should do first on Christmas morning before opening our gifts?

December 22
Balthazar and the Burning Balm

According to tradition, Balthazar, the second of the three wise men came from Arabia bringing a gift of frankincense, which is basically sap from a tree that has a very sweet smell when burned. Traditionally frankincense was burned during high times of worship. By offering to Jesus this sweet perfume, Balthazar and the other wise men were letting everyone know that this baby was more than just a human. He was someone that deserved to be worshipped. He was God on Earth.

Today, in our culture, we usually don't burn something as a sign of worship to God. But the Bible does tell us that our prayers and worship are like a sweet fragrance to God (Rev. 5:8). That is why we sing worship songs in church. That is part of why we pray together. We are in a sense offering a sweet smell to God.

Balthazar got it right by offering the frankincense to Jesus. But so often many people today get it wrong. We go to church and watch church happen before our eyes without fully participating in the experience of worshipping God. Perhaps there are things in our life that are taking our focus off of God or perhaps we are easily distracted. Whatever the reason, we fail to send that sweet aroma to God through our prayers and worship.

Christmas is a great time of year to worship God. It signifies the beginning of Jesus's time on earth and therefore can be a new beginning of our time to worship Him. Just remember worship is not just about singing. It's about living. It's about making right choices. It's about obeying what God tells us we should do. We worship God when we help others especially when we sacrifice what belongs to us in order to help someone else.

Family Discussion

What are some of your favorite smells?

When you walk into a room that has a nice smell, how does that make you feel?

Why do you think God liked the smell of burning frankincense?

What are some ways that we as a family can worship God?

December 23
Melchoir and the Mark of Myrrh

The third wise man traditionally came from Persia and was known by the name of Melchoir. Whereas the other two wise mean brought gifts that would make sense to most people – gold given to royalty and frankincense given to God, the third gift of Myrrh at first glance probably seemed rather strange to Mary and Joseph. At that time, Myrrh was used to embalm dead bodies. It had to have been strange to see a new born baby given something that is usually reserved for dead people. But in God's plan for Jesus, it made perfectly good sense. After all, Jesus came to earth as a baby so that one day He would die for our sins. Melchoir's gift showed that the wise men understood that the new born king had been sent to earth so that He would die and save the world.

Though it is true that during the Christmas season, we prefer to focus on the beauty of the Christmas story and the innocence of what a newborn baby symbolizes, there is still a subtle emphasis on sacrifice seen all around us. Almost every store we enter during the Christmas season will have someone ringing the Salvation Army bell, asking us to sacrifice just a little bit to help others. Churches everywhere unite together, asking their congregation to give money or buy items to help the underprivileged people around the world. Many sacrifice their time to volunteer in some kind of ministry while others band together to sing Christmas carols to those in nursing homes.

So even now, just as Myrrh was given as a symbol of the sacrifice that Jesus would make, we find ways to sacrifice a part of ourselves each Christmas season. Let me encourage you this Christmas season to find ways to demonstrate sacrifice at the same time that we are

Rockin' Around the Christmas Tree and experiencing *Joy to the World.* You may just find out the truth of what Jesus knew all the time. It really is better to give than to receive.

Family Discussion

List all the ways that you have seen people sacrificing to help others during this Christmas season.

Why do you think, especially during Christmas, that it is important for us to demonstrate sacrifice?

In what ways have you sacrificed of yourself during this Christmas season?

Tomorrow is Christmas Eve and the next day is Christmas day. Can you think of a way that you could demonstrate sacrifice to either your family or other people in these final few days of the Christmas season?

December 24
Mary: Cherish The Moment

For Mary, that first Christmas must have been a very strange night. First she delivered her baby in a stable surrounded by an assortment of animals. Jesus probably was no more than a couple of hours old when suddenly a group of shepherds entered the stable to worship her baby.

The Bible tells us that Mary took in everything that was going on around her and she cherished every moment, locking it into her mind so she could remember it forever. She memorized what the face and actions of the baby Jesus showed as He lay in the manger. She made sure she got a good look at every animal in the stable so she could always remember who and what had witnessed the most famous and glorious birth of all time. She would never forget the smile of Joseph as he looked at his newborn step son and prayed for God's wisdom to help him be the earthly father of God's Son. And she probably memorized the names and faces of the shepherds that were surprise visitors to the stable that night.

And now thousands of years later, those very things that Mary cherished in her heart, every Christmas season, we still cherish today. What better way to cherish the Christmas story than to read Luke 2:1-20.

Below, you will find the Christmas story in the King James Version. Should you want to use a different translation, feel free to read it from your own Bible.

And it came to pass in those days, that there went out a decree from Caesar Augustus that all the world should be taxed.

² (And this taxing was first made when Cyrenius was governor of Syria.)

³ And all went to be taxed, every one into his own city.

⁴ And Joseph also went up from Galilee, out of the city of Nazareth, into Judaea, unto the city of David, which is called Bethlehem; (because he was of the house and lineage of David:)

⁵ To be taxed with Mary his espoused wife, being great with child.

⁶ And so it was, that, while they were there, the days were accomplished that she should be delivered.

⁷ And she brought forth her firstborn son, and wrapped him in swaddling clothes, and laid him in a manger; because there was no room for them in the inn.

⁸ And there were in the same country shepherds abiding in the field, keeping watch over their flock by night.

⁹ And, lo, the angel of the Lord came upon them, and the glory of the Lord shone round about them: and they were sore afraid.

¹⁰ And the angel said unto them, Fear not: for, behold, I bring you good tidings of great joy, which shall be to all people.

¹¹ For unto you is born this day in the city of David a Saviour, which is Christ the Lord.

¹² And this shall be a sign unto you; Ye shall find the babe wrapped in swaddling clothes, lying in a manger.

¹³ And suddenly there was with the angel a multitude of the heavenly host praising God, and saying,

¹⁴ Glory to God in the highest, and on earth peace, good will toward men.

¹⁵ And it came to pass, as the angels were gone away from them into heaven, the shepherds said one to another, Let us now go even unto Bethlehem, and see this thing which is come to pass, which the Lord hath made known unto us.

¹⁶ And they came with haste, and found Mary, and Joseph, and the babe lying in a manger.

¹⁷ And when they had seen it, they made known abroad the saying which was told them concerning this child.

¹⁸ And all they that heard it wondered at those things which were told them by the shepherds.

¹⁹ But Mary kept all these things, and pondered them in her heart.

²⁰ And the shepherds returned, glorifying and praising God for all the things that they had heard and seen, as it was told unto them.

Family Discussion

What are some of the memories of Christmas that you will always cherish?

What is your favorite part of the Christmas story and why?

Why do you think Mary cherished every minute of that night, including the visit by the shepherds?

What are some of the things in our lives that God wants us to hold on to and cherish?

December 25
Christmas Morning
Jesus: God's Greatest Gift

Traditionally around the world, Christmas morning is one of the most exciting mornings of the year. As a kid, I always had trouble sleeping the night before as I lay in bed anticipating what was wrapped under the Christmas tree. Would I get that special gift that I had been wanting? What surprise gifts were there that I had no idea I would be getting?

Now as an adult, I still eagerly look forward to Christmas morning, but instead of viewing that morning through my eyes, I love to view it through the eyes of my son. I enjoy that partly because it reminds me of my own childhood and partly because as an adult, I have learned that it really is better to give than to receive.

Giving is part of God's character. We all receive from God throughout the year. For some, He gives in financial ways and for some He gives in the form of health. Others He grants them peace and contentment and still others receive spiritual blessings. There is no limit to the kinds of gifts God gives to His children.

However, without a doubt, the greatest gift God has ever given to the world was His Son, Jesus Christ. All the other great gifts God has given to us would not mean a thing had He not chosen to send Jesus into this world. Because Jesus was given to this world as a baby and grew up as a perfect man, He was able to die to pay for our sins so that we would have the opportunity to live forever with God in Heaven. Jesus truly is the gift that lasts forever.

But just as it is with any gift with our name on it that we see under the tree on Christmas morning, God's gift of Salvation that He offers through Jesus will do us no good if we do not take the gift and open it.

Think of the best Christmas present you ever received. You know the one. The one that you could not put down. The one that you had to play with or use all the time. Maybe it was the gift that made you the happiest of all the gifts you have ever received. What would have happened had you never unwrapped that gift and claimed it as your own? You would have missed out on hours and hours, perhaps years of enjoyment. All because you were given a gift that you never took.

That is the way God's Greatest Gift is for us today. He offers an eternity in Heaven to us if we would just take the gift of His Son and make it our own. It is a gift that sits in front of us to take. Don't push it away and miss out on years of a joyful life through Christ while on earth and an eternity of glory in Heaven.

Family Discussion

What is your favorite Christmas gift of all time?

Have you accepted God's greatest gift of Jesus in your life?

For those who are already Christians, think past your salvation. What does it mean to you today that God is still offering you the gift of His Son?

Other Devotionals By Steve Biddison

10 Minutes to Better Living: Daily Applications From the Life of Christ

In just 10 minutes a day, you can be on your way to living a better life? This easy to read daily devotional is filled with simple truths and practical applications from the life of Christ.

Join me on a journey as we study our Savior through His day to day life and find truths that you can immediately put into action.

10 minutes and a willing heart to follow God is all it takes to help put you on the road to better living.

31 Days To Becoming a Man of God: Practical Life Lessons From the Men in the Bible

31 Days to Becoming a Man of God is a devotional series designed to be a short daily reading that will delve beyond the surface stories concerning the men in the Bible and cut straight into some very valuable and practical applications that husbands and fathers (as well as men in general) of the 21st century need in order to become strong men of God. This is not designed as a deep Theological book, but rather a devotional that looks at the examples (both good and bad) of the men that grace the pages of the Bible

For More From Steve Biddison, visit
www.stevebiddison.wordpress.com

Email: stevebiddisonbooks@aol.com

Twitter: @stevebiddison

Facebook Author Page: Steve Biddison Books

CPSIA information can be obtained at www.ICGtesting.com
Printed in the USA
LVOW05s0105281114

415860LV00018B/562/P